T0069157

A History of Clouds

THE GERMAN LIST

A History of Clouds
99 Meditations

HANS MAGNUS ENZENSBERGER

TRANSLATED BY MARTIN CHALMERS AND ESTHER KINSKY

LONDON NEW YORK CALCUTTA

This publication was supported by a grant
from the Goethe-Institut India

Seagull Books, 2018

Die Geschichte der Wolken. 99 Meditationen
© Suhrkamp Verlag, Frankfurt am Main 2003

Translations © Martin Chalmers, Esther Kinsky, 2010

First published in English by Seagull Books, 2010

ISBN   978 0 8574 2 579 9

British Library Cataloguing-in-Publication Data

A catalogue record for this book is available
from the British Library

Printed at Graphic Print, Calcutta

A History of Clouds
99 Meditations

HANS MAGNUS ENZENSBERGER

TRANSLATED BY MARTIN CHALMERS AND ESTHER KINSKY

LONDON NEW YORK CALCUTTA

**GOETHE
INSTITUT**

This publication was supported by a grant
from the Goethe-Institut India

Seagull Books, 2018

Die Geschichte der Wolken. 99 Meditationen
© Suhrkamp Verlag, Frankfurt am Main 2003

Translations © Martin Chalmers, Esther Kinsky, 2010

First published in English by Seagull Books, 2010

ISBN   978 0 8574 2 579 9

Printed at Graphic Print, Calcutta

It is the wisdome of Cats to whet their Claws in meditation of the next Rat they are to encounter.

Andrew Marvell, *The Rehearsal Transposed* (1672)

Contents

I

Remembering the Poignant Moment / 3

Sins of Omission / 4

Invariably / 6

Division of Labour / 8

Lost / 9

Genetics / 10

Underground Station Wittenbergplatz / 11

After-Dinner Speech at an Engagement / 12

Obscure Camera / 13

My Wife's Merits / 14

Nude Shot / 15

Temperatures / 16

In Semi-Darkness / 17

Surfaces / 18

Thunderstorm in Winter / 19

Surprises / 20

Profane Revelation / 21

Thirst / 22

To the Spoilsport / 23

II

The Way Out / 27

Before Techno and After / 28

For Max Sebald / 30

The Copy / 31

Low Notes in Liepāja / 33

A Cosy Evening / 35

One Day / 36

Sans-papier. Boulevard de Port-Royal, March 1999 / 37

Peace Talks / 38

Motivational Research / 39

Poem in Parentheses / 40

Child Soldiers / 42

Interference / 43

The Energy Field of the Dead / 44

Stars / 45

III

Malfunction / 49

Further Cause for Complaint / 51

All Kinds of Grievances / 52

Astronomical Sunday Sermon / 54

Little Theodicy / 55

Ever Briefer Conversations / 56

Concerning the Question What is More Blesséd / 57

At Times / 58

Spectators / 59

So Much for Good International Relations / 60

Lovely Days in Xinjiang / 61

Pakse / 62

Better Prospects / 64

A Little Swan Song to Mobility / 66

Power of the Keys / 67

IV

Also One Half of Life / 71

The Party / 72

Pet / 73

Voices / 74

The Buttons / 76

The Instruments / 78

An Earth-Coloured Ditty / 79

Fish Knives and Ideas / 80

19 Berggasse / 81

Will and Representation / 83

A Pity / 84

Tripp's Cabinet of Curiosities / 86

Words Fail Me / 87

The Words, the Words / 88

Parliamentary / 90

The Autobiographer / 92

Little Night Music on a Hotel Toilet / 93

Interim Report / 94

Superfluous Elegy / 95

A Small Contribution Towards Reduction / 96

V

Final Remarks on Certainty / 99

It Might Escape Some Souls / 100

Swans / 101

Credit / 102

The Advantages of the Finite / 104

Theory of Names / 106

Gaps in Our Knowledge / 107

Problems Falling Asleep / 108

Orders of Magnitude / 109

Take Note, Bishop Berkeley / 110

Questions for the Cosmologists / 112

Augurs / 113

If You Believe It / 114

Astrolabe / 115

Chemistry of Transparence / 117

Lead / 118

Climate Machine / 120

Atomic Weight 12.011 / 121

VI

A History of Clouds / 125

I

Remembering the Poignant Moment

The morning of regret seizing your joints like lumbago;
the day when you made a fool of yourself for ever and a
day;
the evening when you're lying on the floor with blood
running from your nose;
the hour in which you discover that for fourteen years
nine months and two weeks you've been mistaken;
the minute when your daughter looks at you as if she
were a stranger;
the moment at which you imagine you feel the tip of
the knife in your back;
the instant when you find the farewell letter on the
kitchen table;
the tenth of a second as the avalanche under your feet is
beginning to slide;
and before and after the unimaginably many moments
without a care.

Translated by Esther Kinsky

Sins of Omission

Yes, I was absent without excuse.
I didn't hurry over,
when the need was greatest.
Let slip love affairs,
a failure at rounders,
never properly learned to swim.

Yes, I avoided
fighting to the last bullet.
I refrained from kissing
the hand of the tramp in brotherhood,
and omitted to water
the neighbour's busy lizzies.

Forgot to confess,
shied away
from improving the world,
never dropped out or in at the right time,
failed to take my pills
three times a day.

Yes, I abstained from
killing people. Yes,

I didn't call.
For the time being I have even
refrained from dying.
Forgive me, if you can.

Or just let it be.

Translated by Martin Chalmers

Invariably

Another one of those loving couples
patiently mauling each other;
yet again the man with the jokes
nobody's laughing at any more;
and she's there too, the woman with the dog
who scares off the whole world with his barking;
the failure in bed—oh yes, him!—
and that other one who's racking his brains
because his sports car exhaust is rusting;
and that one, incredibly, who doesn't want to pay;
or—dear me!—the toneless grandchild
with the warped and drooping bottom lip,
and the killer, look!
how he's going on about his defeat,
back then, six hundred years ago;
It is the hot flush of remembered embarrassment,
the fear of the next stomach cramp,
the long awaited kiss of betrayal—
all of it rises punctually
like a roly-poly man, comes back
like the telephone bill and the moon.
Woe on us! Again and again the same boring shock,
the wretched recognition

when the box pops open
and old Jack shoots up into our faces.

Translated by Esther Kinsky

Division of Labour

Everything you can't do:
Land a fully-laden jumbo jet,
demonstrate Mordell's Theorem,
knit—others do it for you,
untalented as you are, dependent
on Blessed Saint Bernadette,
the prison governor, the man
with the insulated pliers, the fortune-teller,
the dustman, the medicine man
and, not least, on Mummy.
They can all do something, contribute
to your maintenance, keep you entertained,
keep you company, whether
you like it or not—and you?

Translated by Martin Chalmers

Lost

Yes, the *Odyssey*! Once, some knew
it by heart, at the very least
a couple of lines. The dry cleaner's
with the Chinese woman is no longer there.
What was that you said? The pneumatic drill
is raising a lot of dust in my ear. And where
has that cloud, glittering so wonderfully
in the oblique light, got to?
Gone! And you, my dear?
Suddenly you're disappointed.
Only a minute ago it seemed
as if you were enchanted! But now
something new is already beckoning
blood-red from the shop window
you float past, where
yesterday the football game was showing,
which ended in a draw.

Translated by Martin Chalmers

Genetics

They say that he with her and she with him did score.
That's obvious. But was that it?
Just sheer coincidence, at midnight or before?

She offered everything she had to give,
he only did the least, or little more,
of what, by Darwin's grace, was up to him.

Was it from need, from love, from malice, or . . . ?
Why, no! They didn't plan for anything.
They made off soon, and either one alone.

They were a pair of two somnambulists.
What was the upshot, once the dice were thrown,
of this setup in its mindlessness?

Was it a Nobody, something of darkness born?
One of the Just, or a monstrosity?
It's true that she with him and he with her did score.

And doing so they really had no other thought.

Translated by Esther Kinsky

Underground Station Wittenbergplatz

Those who descend towards you, down
to the quotidian Hades
on the escalator, this old man,
wrapped up in himself with his morose heart,
and the crumpled woman,
muttering something bitter to herself—

they too were once aflame,
once, sometime, lost to the world,
overjoyed, radiant
and boisterous, or not?
How did it happen? Since when? And why?
Outside the snow too has turned

to slush again.

Translated by Martin Chalmers

After-Dinner Speech at an Engagement

This self, a container, which,
as long as no one opens it,
appears compact, smooth
as a Kinder egg,
almost appetizing. Only inside,
there it's dark. Who knows
what's waiting for you there.
Obsessions no doubt,
rusty habits,
incomprehensible fears,
second-hand tricks,
childish desires.
That you want to have it,
this gift box,
borders on a miracle.

Translated by Martin Chalmers

Obscure Camera

The woman over there, in front of you,
against the light, vague
her lips and eyes,
a revenant. Only—
who and when, you wonder,
where is she from,
what is it she's leaving unsaid,
what is it she's reproaching me with?

In a cloud of darkness
she stands there, motionless.
Blinded by too much light,
too much forgetting,
you sit in front of her
on this naked chair.
You do not see.
You are being seen.

Translated by Esther Kinsky

My Wife's Merits

My wife's merits are too numerous
for an A4 sheet of paper.
She is multicellular, with rustling hair
thriving wonderfully at night, in her sleep.
Each and every hair is dear to me. She's well provided
with soft spots. Whenever her nostrils
vibrate slightly, I know: she's thinking.
How often she thinks, and how inarbitrarily she lives!
I know she can curl her tongue,
play footsie. When she laughs or grumbles
a new wrinkle appears at her mouth,
which I like. She's not entirely white,
is of more than one colour. Her breaths, too,
are numerous, not to mention
the manifold souls in her breast.
I am amazed that here,
where I happen to be, is where she usually is.

Translated by Esther Kinsky

Nude Shot

The thunder in the August night woke me,
but you threw off the sheet in your sleep,
dreamless, unmoved by the electric storm.
Magnesium flashes dazzle your closed lids.
A violet whiteness glows on your breathing hips,
while a thousand times over the dancing water patters
on the roof.

Translated by Martin Chalmers

Temperatures

There are temperatures no thermometer will measure,
only skin can distinguish them:
The lukewarm baby breath smelling of buttermilk,
the cool waft of the peaches from the fridge,
the reddish rash of anger driving the measles into our face,
and the cold flower of frost burning on the child's
        curious tongue;
furthermore the feverish glow of jealousy in our fingertips,
burning shame flooding the brain,
and—unparalleled at any other time or point in our
galaxy:
the two warmths of the sleepers snuggling up to each
        other in bed.

Translated by Esther Kinsky

In Semi-Darkness

When she's lying there, so entirely
of this world as a cow or a cat,
without intention or regret,
in the semi-darkness a halo
hovers around her shimmering skin.

You can sense it, feel it,
when you're close enough to her,
this soft radiation
in the more distant glow of infrared.
A Fourier transform
No one will decipher.

It is only a breath,
touching you more deeply
than the touch,
and not to know why—
perhaps that is happiness.

Translated by Esther Kinsky

Surfaces

With your eyes closed
you grope, sense something furry,
or is it velvet, or china?
Here you touch on something that is grooved,
porous or oily, coarse, slippery,
no, this is rather grained,
that could be glass, or rubber,
it's yielding, waxy, cracked,
and now it suddenly feels sticky,
repulsive! Something else is grainy,
like silk, no, it's like sandpaper,
floury, matt, damp—give up!
For your few words are dull,
unreliable, helpless, blind—
more miserable than your fingertips,
which know their way around the world
where you blunder, is your stammering.

Translated by Esther Kinsky

Thunderstorm in Winter

When the air turns white
and sight grows blind
the sky bangs and flashes
the lights go out in the offices
and only the sirens of the fire brigade
pierce the whirling curtain
pushing bright drifts in front,

worries, business, urgent matters
disappear for a quarter of an hour
and you look out,
free of thoughts at last,
into the blindingly darkened world.

Translated by Esther Kinsky

Surprises

A magpie splays its feathers on the railing.
There's fragrance or a bang at every street corner.
You never step into the same lift twice.
This field of flowering rape, pulling past the
dining car window—
as if you had never seen such a yellow sea before!
Or that cloud there above the Pantheon,
the overpowering smell of tar, rising
black and hot into the sky, the snow-
flake on a woman's downy arm—
something that was never there before. Is it only
the art of forgetting, which allows you
to notice, how new your mistakes,
your illuminations are, eternal beginner,
which, as long as you can remember, you are.

Translated by Martin Chalmers

Profane Revelation

Snow white tabernacle,
even the eternal drunkard
will find mercy before you,
in the twinkling of an eye you absolve
the sinning woman
and illuminate the sleepless,
kneeling in the brightness of your radiance
before you, nightly consolation
for the thirsty, sweet helper in need
of all who suffer hunger.

Full of promise you open up
to the needy, you tiny
icy garden of Eden!
With manna thou blessest the pilgrim,
with fresh peaches, grapes,
shiny cherries and wine.
Altar or refrigerator:
Given the choice,
many a pious belief,
believe me, would falter.

Translated by Esther Kinsky

Thirst

She stretches, yawns,
splays her toes,
exposes the tiny
soft pricks
on her tongue,
while the television
splutters and laughs
as if out of its mind.
Then, like a Turk
saying No, she nods
upwards, a dozen times,
throwing the milk
into her rosy maw.

Translated by Esther Kinsky

To the Spoilsport

Euphoria, what vanity
without reason or rhyme.
Well, it will always be
alien to you, my friend,
for it needs no theory.
Happy—you said—that's
for cows as well, and sheep,
this petty happiness
is just a boring flat idea.
You're a poor bastard,
mon ami,
but that you'll never see.

Translated by Esther Kinsky

II

The Way Out

There isn't always one,
but yet
more often than you thought.
Of course, only when
you've come to a dead end
do you find it,
in a narrow secret place,
where you can slip through, the back door.

On the other side
you stand dazzled in the open air.
Hard to believe:
on this freshly painted day
history stands still,
the old story.
No one is bellowing.
Until the next time.

Translated by Martin Chalmers

Before Techno and After

Herr von Eichendorff
didn't shoot himself.
Herr von Eichendorff
didn't take coke, got by without
duels and one night stands.
Herr von Eichendorff
spoke fluent Polish.
His ambitions were modest.
Herr von Eichendorff—
weak lungs, civil servant
in Prussian ministries
for thirty years—
dreamt of French horns
in his office, was good
and good for nothing,
lived inconspicuously, died
and left behind a few lines,
more durable than the crumbling bricks
of Lubowitz, nowadays
Rzeczpospolita Polska,
in the deaf ears of our children:
only a couple of lines,
which one day,
when they retire,

will perhaps allow
them to feel
something soft, unknown,
which was once called melancholy.

Translated by Martin Chalmers

For Max Sebald

Who touched us,
who seemed to have come from afar
to the sinister, unhomely homeland.
Little kept him here.
Nothing but the search for traces
with a divining rod of words
which twitched in his hand.
He followed it across burnt earth and burial sites
even as far as the *raving madness*
on Suffolk heaths.
Is this the promis'd land?

Darkness had fallen early,
yet he went on,
intrepid in every nightmare, no
matter how hard the going.
That the dust grew light for him,
we know only from three lines:
So soundlessly I glided
hardly brushing a wing
high up above the earth . . .

Translated by Martin Chalmers

The Copy

When Steinar Pétursson, a gaunt man
from Borgarnes in distant Iceland,
carpenter by trade,
arrived in Copenhagen by packet steamer
a good hundred years ago,
he saw a wonderful machine.

It was a band-saw
of gleaming steel.
Yet when Steinar discovered what it cost,
as much as one hundred and fifteen
sheep by Faxaflói Bay,
he closed his eyes.

He ran his fingers
over belt pulley, hand wheel and stop.
For four days on the packet
Steinar Pétursson was silent.
At home he took the hardest wood
and shut himself into his workshop.

His work, a band-saw made entirely of wood,
only the blade is iron,
can still be seen today, among spinning wheels,

stuffed puffins
and old birth spoons, in a corner
of the local museum at Borgarnes.

Translated by Martin Chalmers

Low Notes in Liepāja

We don't know what he looked like,
but I imagine
him to be small, stocky,
his hair iron gray, his hand
slender but firm.
He must have come by ship
with his planes and mallets,
bars of tin and lead, with the ivory
for the draw stops,
Heinrich Andreas Contius
from distant Halle.

The ice floes cracked
on Lake Libau.
Spring in Kurland is hard.
There, between two Turkish wars,
he began to build
a tremendous organ:
Echo division, upper chest, small chest, main manual,
and the pedals. He pulled out all the stops: Vox coelestis
and Portunal,
Bourdon, Flautino, Gedackt and Bombard.
The Viola d'amore was only
added a century later.

Tsars, knights, Red and White Guards
marched past, Legionnaires, Chekists,
Sonderkommandos came and went.
Holy Trinity Church has survived,
the biggest mechanical organ in the world.
Only the chimes have vanished without trace.
But when the largest of seven thousand
pipes, the Sub Bourdon, sounds,
thirty-two feet high,
heaven and earth tremble.

Translated by Martin Chalmers

A Cosy Evening

Peace at last! No one there,
a colour supplement idyll.
If only there weren't the books,
whispering something in your ear
about vultures and rockets,
on the wall the dumb wood
on which for centuries
a painted Troy has been burning,
and this black box,
which can't wait
to show you,
between twitching Go-Go girls
and toilet cleaner
the same massacre again and again.
It can't be healthy, can it?

Translated by Martin Chalmers

One Day

Rambo, overcome by the fever of good nature, feeds
his last yoghurt to a baby;
the coxman succumbs to the charms of monogamy;
Dr Frankenstein (MIT) deletes his source code
and goes to work for the Red Cross in Burundi;
with a sigh of relief the miser throws his treasure,
a collection of letters from the front, into the fire;
the tyrant is fed up to the back teeth with all the torturing,
and henceforth prefers growing marrows. However,

the others go on just as before.

Translated by Martin Chalmers

Sans-papier.
Boulevard de Port-Royal, March 1999

Calm conversation with the poet on the fourth floor,
snowed under his manuscripts,
periodicals on the table, along the wall
silent classics, Bible paper, durable
and thin as onion-skins.

Drumming on the boulevard outside,
police vans, loudspeakers, dancers,
crying children and women
like queens in African robes,
trying to find a scrap of paper.

Translated by Martin Chalmers

Peace Talks

Being offended is everything.
'Just because we're so poor.'
'Just because we defend ourselves.'
'Just because you
don't like our gods.'
'Just because you are envious.'
'What on earth have you got against us
just because of a couple of bombs?'
'Why do you get so upset
just because we always win?'
'It's not our fault,
if we're offended.'

Resentment is always right.
Revenge is a pleasure too.
It would be best, if you would
fall upon each other, until
there's no one left
to be offended.

Translated by Martin Chalmers

Motivational Research

Unfortunately I have no choice but to kill you,

☐   because you refuse to speak Basque
☐   because the bank has blocked my overdraft
☐   because of daddy
☐   because I can't bear the sight of unveiled women
☐   because the rich get on my wick
☐   for the sake of the Dear Lord
☐   because you won't give me any money for the next shot
☐   because you're not Catholic enough/much too Catholic
☐   because I'm offended
☐   because of mummy
☐   because you're always looking at me funny
☐   because I ticked the wrong boxes in the exam and failed
☐   because I hear voices
☐   and anyway. Just because.

I thank you for your time.

(Tick as applicable *before taking action!*)

Translated by Martin Chalmers

Poem in Parentheses

Herewith [said the voice (quietly) (not thundering)
(from above)] it shall be (in keeping with the General
Terms of Business)
confirmed to Mr A. A. (albeit grudgingly) (yet
((halfway)) in recognition
of his {(((as rumour has it) well known)) ((albeit
vague))} merits)
(by [said the (inconspicuous) voice {and it sounded
tired (as the voice of an ((asthma-ridden)) old man)}]
the Court of Last Judgement) that he (occasionally)
{in consideration of all (mitigating ((or, esp.
aggravating)))

circumstances
(with the exception of those) [continued the voice
(growing ever fainter)]
(which ((for certain reasons) remained {{more or less}}
unclear))) (and apart from ((scattered
{{not particularly noteworthy}} dirty tricks))))}
has (actually) always
[and these words were uttered (almost) inaudibly]
displayed a (relatively)

correct
and (almost) human behaviour.

Translated by Esther Kinsky

Child Soldiers

How it scratched, the mouldy-green
rough uniform cloth
on bare skin.
Not yet seventeen,
the eagerness for death
shining metallically
from his blue eyes.
A Werwolf, hanged
in the hot May of '45
on a market square in Franconia.

An example to all those today
who have never heard
of him and his like.
Other promises,
other lies and skies,
rags of a different colour,
yet the same smell of oil,
nitrocellulose and fear,
the same zeal to put an end
to others and oneself.

Translated by Martin Chalmers

Interference

Hope would be saying too much,
but when a double rainbow appears
over the ravaged villages,
then, for a few minutes,
they lower their knives
and watch as it slowly
fades before their blood-
shot eyes.

Translated by Martin Chalmers

The Energy Field of the Dead

As long as there are cemeteries, stelae, tumuli,
everything is not lost.
Even in ruins life goes on,
buried under weathered
sheds, guiltily innocent,
takes its revenge, radiates
invisibly, defends itself, helps,
keeps going, perhaps to the end of the world,
and perhaps not.

Translated by Martin Chalmers

Stars

for Adam Zagajewski

Every year with astronomical precision they come up
again.
The creeper here is called, I think, moneywort,
and the tiny plant there is wall pepper.
So much that's yellow and fades so soon.
Of those that are very far from us,
in the cold, it's said that they burn up
like birthday sparklers.
When the wind drops, some hang limp
from the flagpoles. One is to be found in the Bible.

When I was small, there were others,
crushed and crooked, and someone must have
sewn them on worn, grey coats.
It wasn't my Aunt Therese,
other aunts sat, the thread in their mouths,
long-sightedly trying to find the eye of the needle.
So many stars. Don't talk about them.
Except that they were yellow. Yellow.
And then they were gone.

Translated by Martin Chalmers

III

Malfunction

O Deus sive natura, evolution,
you probably didn't anticipate that.
Yes, it can happen to anyone.
If one's as powerful as that—
some coincidence perhaps, and already
there's a creature standing
on two feet, starting to talk,
even worse—to think!
Of course, in the beginning
they still plead,
smoke rises from the altars,
but no sooner do they have more or less
enough to eat, than they get cocky.
Hans Peter Grauke from Fulda,
to name just one,
lurking outside the disco
with his new hunting knife,
not a suitable case for therapy, or Höllreuther,
virologist, with a sideline as saviour of the world:
Billions saying me-me-me.
Mad, whatever they get into their heads.
They get everything mixed up.

And yet you, dear evolution, had
Arranged it all so wonderfully well.

Translated by Martin Chalmers

Further Cause for Complaint

That everything was much worse,
once, here at least—
cooped up in one's own country,
in one's own coal cellar,
Struggle as Inner Experience,
puberty on ration cards,
and the murderous bad breath
of some dictator—
no one wants to know any more.

Instead, go on whining
about cancelled Christmas bonuses,
the decline in moral standards, and the poor food
on the charter flight to Mombasa.

Damned
to doing nicely,
each one avoids
letting out
this dirtiest of all secrets.

Translated by Martin Chalmers

All Kinds of Grievances

Just one step, and an avalanche breaks free.

He who is full cannot remember being hungry.
The airplane's disappearing from the radar screen.
The tramp doesn't regard the winners fondly.

Sunday's child gives himself up to the police—
just one more loony and as such redundant—
and takes the liberty to shout from jail his great relief.

The terrorist is proud of his credentials.
In fairy tales the cup that overflows tastes sweet.
A child molester's looking forward to confession.

Many a moral guardian contemplates:
A line of coke and I would suffer less depression,
my nerves are really in a dreadful state.

Athletes dozing in old people's care homes
Are tied by nurses to their bed to vegetate.
A last word shall be said now in the boardroom.
The muscle flexers hide away and weaklings plan
a riot. Prophets abound, and all the while a snoring
sleeper is dreaming that he'll take revenge.

And what are the director's thoughts, or seem to be?
No panic please, no lust for fear, he recommends,
and then declares: all this is just routine.

Translated by Esther Kinsky

Astronomical Sunday Sermon

When talk turns to our misfortunes—
starvation murder manslaughter etc.—
Granted! A madhouse!
But please permit me
to remark in all modesty
that all in all
it's quite a favourable planet
on which we find ourselves,

a rose arbour
compared to Neptune
(minus 212 degrees centigrade,
wind speeds of more than 600 mph
and a helluva lot of methane
in the atmosphere).
Just so you know, that elsewhere
it's much less comfortable.

Translated by Martin Chalmers

Little Theodicy

First you invent Him,
then you try
to devour each other,
mutually,
in His Name,
and then some
poor vicar's son shows up
from Saxony
and declares Him dead.

Who'd be surprised
that His interest
in such pompous asses
is limited?
Now you are offended.
just because God is yawning
without regard for you.

Translated by Esther Kinsky

Ever Briefer Conversations

'Blessed is the man that walketh not
in the counsel of the ungodly . . .'
One tactfully changes the subject.

'The meaning of life . . .'
Embarrassing gaffe!

'It is necessary to overthrow all
conditions in which man
is an enslaved being . . .'
Everyone yawns, looks the other way, laughs.

Genomes, on the other hand, made to measure,
immortality on a hard disk—
oh science! Ecstasy! Euthanasia!

Sometimes one is happy enough
that a few of the stick-in-the-muds
among the younger folk
still have a few questions.

Translated by Martin Chalmers

Concerning the Question What is More Blesséd

The world has given you, Monsignore,
you, old mate, and you, Madame Sans Papier,
so much,
any amount of air, toys,
tap water and fruit,
the occasional chat in bed,
tons of petrol,
sleeping pills, soap operas
and extras galore—

boundless, indeed,
exceeding all limits.
It goes too far, old friend.
It's beyond your ken,
Maestro. The world has given you
so much,
that an old bum like you
cannot possibly ever return,
can you?

Translated by Esther Kinsky

At Times

When you meet someone
who is smarter or more stupid than you—
don't make too much of it.
The ants and the gods,
believe me, feel just the same.
That there are more people in China,
say, than San Marino,
is no misfortune.
Most people, no doubt, are
blacker or whiter than you.
At times you're a giant,
like Gulliver, or a dwarf.
Somewhere or other you're always discovering
an even more radiant beauty,
someone even worse off.
You're mediocre,
luckily. Accept it!
Seven degrees centigrade more
or less on the thermometer—
and you would be beyond saving.

Translated by Martin Chalmers

Spectators

Reverently we come to a halt
like a herd of cows,
here, on the hard shoulder.
The smouldering wreckage we gape at,
the ambulance crew, the cameras
we gape at, absent-mindedly
we gape at the dying.

Only the cows over there on the hill,
a stone's throw away in the clover,
disregard us, chew,
do not raise their heavy heads,
chew, lost in thought,
until we get in, slamming the doors,
and just drive on.

Translated by Esther Kinsky

So Much for Good International Relations

Noise in the worldwide radio:
crackling and tongue-clicking, coughing.
All the languages you'll never speak.
Nobody really knows how many there are.
With a thousandth of them mapped in,
you'd be a polyglott.
Chinook, Beluchi, Rapankaka:
No miracle of Pentecost in sight.
You understand nothing,
never understood much,
and now it's a little late
to begin.

Translated by Esther Kinsky

Lovely Days in Xinjiang

Nowhere is poverty as rich
as on the big Sunday bazar of Kash.
Some eighty thousand, for sure,
the hats trimmed
with marmot fur,
and silk brocade overflowing with gold.
A luxury thriving only in the desert:
The mules' harness adorned
with pink rosettes, and the croup
with a dozen little bells,
the women in wild colours which no one
else would dare wear.
If only it weren't so miserably poor,
this profusion—how lovely would it be
there, on the big Sunday bazar of Kash.

Translated by Martin Chalmers

Pakse

These people with their sunglasses,
their lotions, their funny hats—
indefatigable, guided
by storytellers,
badgering them
with tedious litanies
and herded by determined shepherds
through crypts and caves,
across fields of ruins and temples
into the most distant mountains.

The awkward and encumbered
from Wuppertal and Chicago.
Heaven knows why
they revere forgotten gods,
for what they seek forgiveness
and miracle healing.

Incomprehensible the hallowed inscriptions,
the bones of the kings vanished,
the tombs empty,
looted are the golden talismans,
the hermit's pillar abandoned.

So they flock
through the desert, through dust and snow.
Pilgrims they are,
albeit of another kind,
without shell, pilgrim's hat, staff and cloak,
and without hope of mercy.

Translated by Esther Kinsky

Better Prospects

One's back to the present,
leaning against the railing,
one sees further,
even in the dark.

Soundlessly behind thick glass
the dreary conversation
of drunk passengers,
the booming bass lines
of the ship's band,
the noise of the engines—
only a faint quivering,
a fleeting smell of diesel oil.

Oh yes, it's full steam ahead.
Now and then the lights
of a vessel going in the opposite direction.
When they've disappeared,
minutes later,
a slight list,
when the bow waves meet.
A rush of turbulence.

So one observes a thing or two,
expects little,
misses nothing.

Translated by Martin Chalmers

A Little Swan Song to Mobility

It was cold in Bogotá.
All the restaurants were shut for the day
in Much-Binding-on-the-Marsh.
In Fiji pouring rain.
Helsinki was booked up.
In Turin the refuse collectors were on strike.
Roadblocks everywhere
in Bujumbura. The silence
over the roofs of Pécs
was something close to panic.
It was least unbearable
under the pear tree
at home.

Translated by Martin Chalmers

Power of the Keys

Back then, on the islands and beyond the woods,
nobody locked themselves in or out.
The kitchen door was always open. But now
we are attached to our key rings.
Bolts, security locks, barriers
like in Manhattan. He is lost, who
misplaces, loses, forgets this rattling
item which alone gives him the right to be
where he belongs. Worn as our own empty pocket,
excluded, homeless we hit
our foreheads against our own front doors.

Translated by Esther Kinsky

IV

Also One Half of Life

At first it's just a tiny number falling prey.
One is run over, the bigmouth from 6b,
or the chubby cousin with her plaits
who had this funny smell is gone,
suddenly gone. Others died in a fire
or were taken away, late at night. Later
bordered letters arrived. Like shadows
it grew, the little group of the absent ones,
and you can't remember this one's
hat and another one's mouth.
And then, one day, the moment comes,
imperceptibly, and passes, when half
of those who fed you, hated, taught
and kissed you have disappeared.

Translated by Esther Kinsky

The Party

No, it was never boring,
despite everything. Enough to eat, usually
(the raspberry tarts—unforgettable),
and then the night sky!
Magnificent! And you, Mama,
changed the nappies in good time.
The shoes were comfortable.
Even the heating worked.
I didn't achieve much.
Didn't kill a dictator,
prevent a massacre.
Was lucky, by and large.
No one tarred me,
rammed a knife into my side.
You patiently put up with
my affairs, my
jokes and my temper.
That was nice of you. The emergency doctor
arrived punctually too. Please,
don't be put out!
The deceased hopes
you will continue to have a good time.

Translated by Martin Chalmers

Pet

My sadness is my hamster.
I don't let it starve. At night
I hear it scraping, scratching, rooting
in its cage. In the morning,
if I'm in a good mood,
I sometimes open the bars.
Then it darts out on pink paws,
seeks me out, looks for food,
investigates me with quivering nostrils.
It sniffs my hand,
until I lose patience,
seize it by the unwilling neck,
so its eyes roll in panic,
and set the squeaking creature down
in its cage. With a click
I slide the bolt
behind it and I'm glad.

Translated by Martin Chalmers

Voices

When the medical officer asks me hypocritically and
by the way if I hear voices, I confess.
What I do not disclose is that it is only one,
always the same one. Yes, it is about me.
Reception is faint. There's a crackling in my ear,
a noise. That's because of the sunspots,
protuberances from a glowing brain.
Or there's the crackle of something long past,
paper rustling with evil ideas.
Perhaps it's an insect touching
the eardrums. It sounds
like the whirring of batwings
in the dark garden of a Roman villa.
A soft trickle as of ashes dribbling
from a shovel. And yet the voice
carries. It booms. What follows
is the echo of an enormous orchestra
in which a soloist abandoned by all reason
has to play all the instruments. In the end
there's nothing but a high note, painful,
as if a moistened finger was running
slowly round the rim of a thin

glass. An ever remoter ringing
that rings and rings and will not let me sleep.

Translated by Esther Kinsky

The Buttons

Buttoning up, unbuttoning,
forever the same thing.
Don't be so buttoned up!
Take some time off!
The bloodied apron,
the summer dress,
lovely! Brass gleams
on the dress uniform.
These black pearls
on her bootees,
coquettish! Iron, rattling
on the convict's uniform.
In the toilet, a thousand times.
Shirt collar,
changing rooms,
hotel rendezvous.
Mother of pearl, polyvinyl.
Millions of buttons.
Where do they all get to?
Now and then one comes off,
rolls to the floor.
Only the shroud

—how practical!—
does without them.

Translated by Martin Chalmers

The Instruments

Eye scissors, penetrometer, urethral catheter—
no one likes to hear the words.
Even the surgeons take care not to
show us the gouge,
that would be unfeeling, the uterine scoop,
it wouldn't be polite, the brain spatula
and the liver retractor. Not until it hurts,
in emergency, do we commit ourselves,
eyes shut, to the male incontinence device,
the blood lancette. Yes, then!
Blessed, we say, all at once
are you, vulva retractor and bone drill,
our only hope,
just before the last rites.

Translated by Martin Chalmers

An Earth-Coloured Ditty

Another poem about death, etc.—
certainly, but what about the potato?
For obvious reasons it's not mentioned
by Horace or Homer, the potato.
But what about Rilke and Mallarmé?
Did it not speak to them, the potato?
Do too few words rhyme
with it, the earth-coloured potato?
It's not too concerned with heaven.
It waits patiently, the potato,
until we drag it out into the light
and throw it onto the fire. The potato
doesn't mind, but could it be
that it's too hot for poets, the potato?
Well, so we'll wait a little while
until we eat it, the potato,
sing about it and then forget it again.

Translated by Esther Kinsky

Fish Knives and Ideas

They are more compact than we are, the objects.
Even when we don't need them any more
they survive on refuse tips,
in cesspits and ruins. Old drawing tools,
rusty fish knives, jagged lids of pocket watches
refuse to perish. Polished and cleaned,
refurbished and desired they resurface,
antiques.
                    Just like obsessions.
Tough and enduring as a strain of bacteria
they survive the decrepit kidneys
of their inventors, ghostlike—the New Man,
the lust for massacres, for God's sake,
the motherland or the apocalypse—
for a few millennia, until they too,
like the fish knife, fall prey to earth,
to rust, to entropy, and follow us
and, like us, only later, much later,
give up the ghost.

Translated by Esther Kinsky

19 Berggasse

The unconscious is our collective lost property office.
Wolfgang Dobereiner

He's grown old, the inspector,
watching over the lost property.
Who handed it in? He won't say.
He draws on the cold cigar
and shows us: the tattered umbrella,
bristling with whalebone spokes,
the Venus statuette, made in Hong Kong,
a pair of forgotten crutches
and the pince-nez with the cracked lens.

The suitcase with the dirty laundry
snaps open. There is the photo album,
in which the deceased fade away once more.
There is the black uniform cap.
There's the false bottom. There lurks
a card game, that spills out at our feet.
The devil, who forces man and woman
together, the falling tower,
the giantess, prising open the lion's jaws.

The old man waits, not speaking. The mantelpiece clock
strikes. Denial is pointless.
Does he not look like the fool,
like the hierophant, or the hermit
with his white beard? Hesitantly,
under his searching gaze,
we draw our card.
The hanged man. Who knows? Perhaps
we've got away with it once more.

Translated by Martin Chalmers

Will and Representation

He thinks he knows what he wants
He gives of his best
He strives He toils
He makes it He climbs
Hats off to his effort
A breeze bore him
A wind

Like this maple leaf
suspended up there
playfully it gets into a spin, wavers
rises up once more
slowly sinks Lies there weak-willed
Rests awhile Rustles
Discolours

Translated by Martin Chalmers

A Pity

Oh, you always paid attention,
took action in good time. The coups
you pulled off, unforgotten, your
grasp of situations feared,
your nose infallible.
Only, to contemplate the idle
rippling of the lake,
to wait while darkness fell,
for that you had no patience.

You just had other worries
and no time for the shiver
of fingertips in hair.
The grey squirrel, astray
in the underground
didn't catch your eye.
As you failed to notice
the scent of love,
which spreads slowly, slowly, to say
nothing at all
of the flickering of the constellations
and the dementia
insinuating itself on tiptoe.

You simply didn't pay attention.
You didn't notice a thing.

Translated by Martin Chalmers

Tripp's Cabinet of Curiosities

Do you see the brush,
the glove, the veined stone?
No, not the pincers on the table there,
not the brush in the painter's hand,
but this glove,
just this seam, these pincers,
this shadow! You're mistaken.
It's no glove, it's art.
Not the art over there,
but the art here.

You rub your eyes and ask,
why are they there,
the stone with all its veins,
these pincers here, this brush,
not that one on the table.

Why? So that you finally
see
what you didn't see.

Translated by Martin Chalmers

Words Fail Me

The magic word, the word of honour, the Word above
all—
I can't bring myself to say it.
In plain words I say to you,
verily, we can get by without them.
Of course, we all struggle to find the right one,
but pst! please no more familiar words, wise words,
just don't breathe another word!
And by the way, this deathly hush
makes me think. In vain
do I wait for the first word,
the word of consent and a word of affection.
Sisters and brothers,
where are you? To be frank,
this silence is beginning to make me nervous,
brothers and sisters. Tell me,
is this your last word?

Translated by Martin Chalmers

The Words, the Words

They seek you out
before you fall asleep,
sit down by your bedside
unbidden.
Where do they all come from?
Perhaps from the underground trains,
from the ether,
from the last century?

A murmuring, droning crowd:
fat words bumping into you,
solemn ones, a mere shadow
of themselves, inconspicuous ones
(oh well, I see, so much for, in that case),
moaning revenants,
words in rags,
pious, obscene, shrill words—
how they swear, flirt and whisper!

It could drive you crazy,
this cloud of midges
milling in the inner ear.
You lash out in all directions,
in vain, sleep

is out of the question.
Turn on the light, rise
and take fright at the silence!

Translated by Esther Kinsky

Parliamentary

Only when the draft is ready,
do I introduce my bill.
Because I am responsible.
Nevertheless, every party
wants to have its say, the
backbenchers too. Hearings,
heckling from the left,
restlessness in the House,
amendments at the last moment.
(These lines for example
were hotly disputed.)
Then the sitting is adjourned.
If need be I appeal
to the arbitration committee.
Then it's put to the vote.
The poem is passed
at a final reading
even before the summer recess. Of course,
at the crucial moment
the chamber is half empty again.
Finally I have the text
made known in the *Federal Poetry Gazette*.

The edition is limited,
the readership select.

Translated by Martin Chalmers

The Autobiographer

He writes about the others,
when he's writing about himself.
He's writing about himself,
when he's not writing about himself.
When he writes, he isn't there.
When he's there, he's not writing.
He disappears, in order to write.
He writes, in order to disappear.
He has disappeared
into what he writes.

Translated by Martin Chalmers

Little Night Music on a Hotel Toilet

The repulsive, and its twin, the beautiful—
they seek us all out, each one differently,
inseparable, always the two of them,
the guardian and the avenging angel.

Pest or spirit of the air, to each his own pair.
At our most delicate nerve strings
they rip and tear.
No victory in sight.

Translated by Esther Kinsky

Interim Report

Sincerest thanks for the pause in transmission,
the pause for a sandwich, the pause for effect—
Quiet please!—in which art
gets stuck in the artist's throat.

Fragile silence, before the century
goes thundering on.
Inconspicuous seconds
of eternity!

At half time,
between two wars,
before the third act,
shortly after the last reminder—

blessed be it,
the short pause for breath
between before
and after life
and demise.

Translated by Esther Kinsky

Superfluous Elegy

Touching, this old tin locomotive,
the violet letters in the bottom drawer
and your most precious object, long ago
forgotten—looks like Made in Thailand—
and the egg-timer, never ever used

and a couple of thousand other things,
lugged up three flights of stairs, diligently,
like crumbs carried off by an ant.
Everything superfluous, take good care of it.
There's not much of you left, if you throw it away.

Translated by Martin Chalmers

A Small Contribution Towards Reduction

The more there is, the more
there is for you to omit,
or is there only an increase
in what is slipping out of your hands?
You almost feel guilty adding something
to what is already
there and getting
more all the time.
The more there is,
the more avoidable most things become. Only
the inconspicuous remains,
as cool as you please.

Translated by Esther Kinsky

V

Final Remarks on Certainty

There are statements.
There are statements that are true.
There are statements that are not true.
There are statements, about which it is impossible to say,
whether they are true or not.
There are statements, about which it is impossible to say,
whether the statement that it is impossible to say,
whether they are true or not,
is true or not,
etc.

Translated by Martin Chalmers

It Might Escape Some Souls

That someone's thinking may be full of sap, like foliage,
sprouting green, sensual, unstoppable,
with many leaves, pinnate, with spades and ribs,
nerves and veins, that it is alive,

until it changes colour, spins to the ground,
withers, perhaps to return, cool, manifold, full of sap,
almost,
but never quite as before, stubborn as foliage,
in the cortex of other brains.

Translated by Esther Kinsky

Swans

That they're white, everyone knows that.
Snow white as the winged coifs of the nuns,
as an egg, an iceberg, snow white,
in a word, as the snow.
So far it's worked out every time
with the four seasons. Always the same thing:
It snows. At worst an avalanche.
Reasonable to suppose,
that things will simply go on as before
with our common catastrophes.

I too knew it all, saw white,
was under the spell of induction,
until one day I stepped out of the house.
It was a wooden shack in Collingwood,
Golden Bay, South Island, and as
the sun rose over the white sand,
the swans flew past out there,
hundreds of swans, majestic
and immaculate, as is their way.
Each one of them was black.

Translated by Martin Chalmers

Credit

Just sheer nothing
is already quite something.
Stomach ache
for metaphysicians.
Inventing zero
was no piece of cake.

And then when
some Indian
had the idea that
something could be less than nothing,
the Greeks came out on strike.

The theologians felt
uneasy too.
A snare, they said,
a temptation of the Devil.

Are these meant to be natural numbers,
exclaimed the doubters,
minus one, minus one billion?
Only someone with money,
and there weren't many of them,
was not afraid:

Debts, write-offs,
double bookkeeping.
The world was discounted.
Arithmetic—a cornucopia.

We all have credit,
said the bankers.
A matter of faith.

Ever since what is less than
nothing is growing ever larger.

Translated by Martin Chalmers

The Advantages of the Finite

The infinite isn't just a bowl of cherries.
If you delve too deep your head will spin,
you'll spin a yarn by telling but the truth.
Poor Achilles, unattainable tortoise!
It never finishes, the infinite,
but that's not all. It has degrees,
infinitely many, one mightier
than the other, from aleph naught to aleph infinity.
As was proved by poor Cantor,
before he died in an insane asylum, and also by
Gödel from Brno, who was even better
versed in it—in the end, he didn't eat anything
any more and starved, curled up like a foetus,
on his mattress. Yes,
even damnation, which is eternal, like
the eternal life, they both should be handled
with only the greatest prudence.
For there's many an advantage to
that which is over being over.
Even our universe, so they say, is finite,
and to nature applies (as to her
older sisters, the goddesses):
Only limitation

will make the mistress shine, for instance
those cherries, over there, in the bowl,
finite in many colours, as they are,
crimson, scarlet, Persian, ruby,
burgundy, poppy and blood red:
They'll be off by tomorrow,
finished and gone. You have to eat them
now or never.

Translated by Esther Kinsky

Theory of Names

My dog, *my* moon crater, *my* duck pond:
All baptized, possession secured,
provided with first names, house, field and nicknames.
Tukkum, for example, Tasso or *Billy's Bar.*
Even the emptiest desert
is called the something desert, Tögrög, Burget Tuyur,
Betpak-Dala. The oceans too are numbered.
The maps are sprinkled with fly-speck.
Only the mosquitoes missed out,
or do you know a midge called Arthur
or George? Comets on the other hand,
nebulae, galaxies. Oh, we'll put our mark on them!
As if we know what Babylon is,
when we call Babylon Babylon.
As if we didn't know: Most of it,
almost all of it, would be there without us.

Translated by Martin Chalmers

Gaps in Our Knowledge

Napoleon in the compound eye of a mosquito
is no more than a vague patch of fog, and conversely
this giant dwarf only notices
the brazen insect that settles
on his nose. The missing man
is declared dead. The end of the world
makes do without observers. Rarely
does our guardian angel make himself known
with a firm handshake. Important things
escape us, soon evaporate.
What counts, what doesn't—
hard to tell the difference. Our brain
is too small to grasp
how small it is. Most everything
comes and goes unnoticed,
untraced and inconsequential as a neutrino.

Translated by Martin Chalmers

Problems Falling Asleep

The class of those problems
which are insoluble
is larger than you think.
No doubt it's growing by the day.
Best not to think about it,
unless you're a cosmologist,
patient, philosopher or marriage counsellor.
Perhaps you would also like to prevent
whole nations falling on one another,
or quite simply hanker after
a *Theory of Everything*. Then that's
something else. Then
we wish you all the best
and now and then your forty winks.

Translated by Martin Chalmers

Orders of Magnitude

Black holes, dark matter,
not meant for our eyes.
The universe prefers conversation
with our apparatuses. Oh yes,
our scientists, they did
make an effort, they see light
in the output of the detectors,
they believe they understand,
how, behind our backs,
Atto and Exa get closer to each other.
And the conclusion is that man
is the measure of mediocrity of all things.
And yet, already as children we discovered,
entirely without a space probe,
how tiny the Milky Way is,
reflected in a drop of water.

Translated by Esther Kinsky

Take Note, Bishop Berkeley

Without a sound the world assures me
that it is there, patiently,
instantly, again and again:
dust flickering in the heat,
the hammer on my thumb,
the cat with its claws,
and also that rushing cloud over there,
a feat of reality
no one else will pull off.

Reality doesn't ask after you,
dear mystics, doesn't offer an opinion
when you once again
claim it to be an illusion.
'Constructivism,'
philosophers' mumblings,
physical reveries,
'a few Quarks, nothing more,'
it just lets it rest.

The world with its cat's eyes
doesn't listen to you.
It lets you talk, patiently,

until it strikes with its claws,
plays with you for a little while
and then forgets you, and remains.

Translated by Esther Kinsky

Questions for the Cosmologists

Whether the light came first,
or perhaps darkness,
whether somewhere there is nothing,
and whether, given you go on like this,
there will be something left at all
of good old matter,
apart from an overdose of mathematics?

Can you tell me
what it is about,
22 dimensions—
or even a few more?—
whether the beyond is a worm hole,
and how many parallel universes
I have to expect?

In awe I listen
to your precise fairy tales,
oh high priests.
So many questions. Whom
should I ask if not
you, the last Mohicans
of metaphysics?

Translated by Esther Kinsky

Augurs

Like their predecessors
they search with the third eye
and ever finer divining rods
for veins and radiation,
tell the future from the innards
of the universe, of mice
and from their own cranium.
Inexorable, silent triumphs!
Who talks of superstition?
Far from it! Entirely without hocus-pocus
they feel their way in the dark,
our harbingers of light, without consideration
for cardinals, tax-payers
and sceptics, almost absent-minded
with cleverness,
until everything we have trusted in:
love affair, consciousness, matter
as well as the sky full of stars
somehow evaporates before our eyes.

Translated by Esther Kinsky

If You Believe It

Some hate being amazed
and then they're amazed
if we find their science boring.
Others don't want to know exactly
and are angry
that we're not interested in their miracles.

Astral body, M-theory, karma, Artificial Intelligence:
I don't know what I prefer:
the promises of the initiated
or the miracles of science.
I listen patiently to the former and the latter,
for hours and for years.

But just don't believe that I believe you!

I can amaze myself.

Translated by Esther Kinsky

Astrolabe

Tympanum, mater and limbus:
past words made of brass.
Who would be able to establish
with alidade, rete and ruler
the altitude of the sun,
Bohemian and Babylonian hours
and the positions of the stars
with their bare hands?

On the planisphere the engraved image
of the celestial globe, azimuth,
almucantar and horizon,
and circling above it a tender web
of thin ribs at whose tips
Aldebaran, Rigel, Antares and Vega
are visible. On the other side
zodiac and shadow square allow
calculation of horoscopes and the height
of towers and peaks.

A calendar, a useful star clock,
an oracle, an analogue computer
sleeping in the museum—scrap metal

to astronomers who don't see anything any more.
Except the discoloured spectre on the screen
and endless columns of numbers.
Ever deeper, into ever more distant galaxies
Penetrates the gaze of science gone blind.

Translated by Esther Kinsky

Chemistry of Transparence

Inconspicuous, it emerges from the soil
out of something grainy
crunching under your feet,
out of something that is ash grey, floury,
chalk white, crumbling,
to be ground, washed,
dipped in cold water,
molten in fire so it will glow and flow,
until the man with the mighty lungs
dips his pipe into the formlessness,
until he makes it dance,
until he spins it, rolls it, pulls it, beats it,
until he breathes his life into it,
until he anneals it,
cuts, smoothes and cools it,
until it congeals, even, tinkling, brittle,
the hardest of all liquids,
shimmering in the light,
transparent as air,
as reason and as the soul,
until it becomes tarnished, blind, cracked,
and crunching it returns
to the earth, inconspicuous.

Translated by Esther Kinsky

Lead

When they still shone, hot from the melting,
the letters were toxic.
Freshly glinting metal
turning blue-gray on contact with the air,
heavy and so soft
that a fingernail can scratch it.
Finely ground it ignites
of its own accord, goes up in smoke. It resides too
in old batteries, lenses, fuses,
shotgun pellets, bright church windows,
gleams in Bohemian glass and crystal.
Pyrotechnicians still use it.
Red lead, white lead: dangerous colours
in old paintings, and at the end of the year
we tell fortunes with it. It collects
in our bones, colics, small,
slow hard pulses, tremors,
dizziness and melancholy,
a saturnine poison that makes us immune
to other, invisible poisons,
in the heavy apron
that the pretty nurse

in the white coat puts on us
when we spit blood.

Translated by Martin Chalmers

Climate Machine

Wrong! It's an old kitchen
and not a machine. It steams,
it boils, it glows and freezes.
She is temperamental and indefatigable, the tempestuous
cook
remains invisible, likes to keep
the lids on her cauldrons for no one to see,
she rinses, steams and roasts us,
thunders and foams. Oh, she's
no different from anybody else
cooks with water
and gas!
                    Poor science,
applying red and blue arrows,
sensors, calculators, probes
to read her tea leaves!
Secret recipes, changing with
the constellations in the sky, depending
on muck, on dirt, on volcanic mush.
Just in time and out of thin air
the cook produces rice, dill, vanilla.
Unpredictably she stirs and stirs the world
with her giant spoon.

Translated by Esther Kinsky

Atomic Weight 12.011

All that is black or white or transparent,
hard or soft, sooty or gleaming, all that
we use to solder, shine, heat and write—
that all of it should be one and the same,

able to enter into 10 (to the power 6) different marriages,
form honeycombs, lattices, chains, rings, tangles,
cords and screws, and that what we breathe is
what we fly with is what we can suffocate on,

and that nothing alive lives without it—
no one except those who want to know all
would have hit upon it, and what we,
who now know it, should do with it—

we do not know.

Translated by Esther Kinsky

VI

A History of Clouds

1

Appearing as they do,
overnight, or out of the blue,
they can hardly be considered
as being born.
Passing away imperceptibly
they have no notion of dying.
And anyway, nobody
can match their transience.

Majestically lonely and white
they rise against a silky blue
or huddle together,
like animals in the cold, collectively
and numb, cluster to form
ink-dark electric disasters,
boom and flash, unmoved,
let hail and water fall.

Then again they boast
of vain feats, change colour,
ape all that is solid.

A game is their history,
unbloodied, older than ours.
They don't need historians,
henchmen, medics, make do
without chiefs, without battles.

Their wanderings high up
are quiet and inexorable.
Nothing bothers them.
Probably they believe
in resurrection, thoughtlessly
happy like me,
lying on my back and
watching them for a while.

2

In case of stress, grief, jealousy, depression
cloud watching is recommended.
With their red and golden evening borders
they surpass Patinir and Tiepolo.
The most fleeting of all masterworks,
harder to count than any herd of reindeer,
don't end up in any museum.

Archaeology of clouds—a science
for the angels. Yes, without clouds
everything living would die. They are inventors:
No fire without them, no electric light.
Indeed, in exhaustion, anger and despair
it is recommended that the eyes
be turned to the sky.

3

The blue sky is blue.
That says everything
about the blue sky.

These flying rebuses however—
although the answer changes all the time,
anyone can decipher them.

They are intangible, so high above,
nebulous. And the gentleness
of their dying! So painless

few things here can match it. The clouds
have no fear, as if they knew:
they'll come into this world again and again.

4

What silken train, this population
of shiny ribs, flakes and veils,
how hurriedly they billow up, those banks,
bales, drums, domes and turrets, and then again
they stall, hang heavy for weeks,
grey and morose—progress
does not occur in the evolution
of clouds. Not a trace
of the fight for survival!
A pinch of dust is enough,
some salt or smoke.
Then they steam,
discharge, pour, flash, hail and snow.
Indeed, they mutate incessantly, over night,
resourceful creatures, non-violent.
No end to their variations, and yet
everything remains as it was.

5

But they have another face too.
Out of anger or exuberance
they bunch together, fist-clenching clusters,
threatening. Exploding in gall-like blackness
the old force erupts from them.
Suddenly everything cracks: sound,
tension, water and ice.

We're caught unawares in our beds
as usual, flee onto the roofs,
teeth chattering, and wait in the dark
with the infant pressed to our chest,
with cage and budgie in our hands,
for the sirens, the rubber dinghy,
the helicopter's distant whirr.

6

Sadly, they don't have
the best reputation.
They're unreliable, it is said.
That there's no knowing even
where they end and where they begin.
Forever this floating and blurring—
thermal, dew point, turbulence—
how infinitely thoughtless, it is said,
and quick to corrupt.
What do they weigh at all?
That is the question.
Moreover, the clouds can
do without us, but not vice versa,
so there's disapproval. Grave accusations,
too grave, perhaps,
for that which lives without gravity.

7

Woe betide us, when they shiver!
In their opaque innards
they produce this white stuff,
myriads of filigree dendrites,
icy, each one different from each other,
as we are, but perfectly regular.

Kepler had no microscope,
but he knew his way,
saw the atomic grid, guessed
its rotational symmetry,
sixty degrees, calculated
its packing density: $\pi / 2\sqrt{3}$.

Sublime crystals. Frailty itself,
tiny, imperceptibly light,
falls on our heads
and, as we sleep, it will
bury many a thing that breathes
under its tons of weight.

8

'The ocean of air can never be to the Naturalist
a subject of unfeeling contemplation,'
said Mr Howard long ago,
while he was weighing pills and powders
on Tottenham Green,
a man inclined to mildness.
Mature, a man of the Enlightenment
and a hunter of clouds, he determinedly
put whatever swept across the sky
in order:
curls, layers and heaps;
he defined the undefined
and limited it, thereby
'putting a stamp on the objects'.
But even christened in Latin,
they continue to do
as they please, the clouds,
not one like the other,
subject to no one. It is difficult
to put a stamp on the sky. Oh,
it is not necessarily
thanks to you, good Howard,
that it clears up, occasionally.

9

Then again they hang low
above us, heavy, for weeks,
and we sit and ponder in their shadow,
that, shot with grey, casts no shadow,
unhappy, until at last
the sleepy blanket parts,
a warm wind blows, all of a sudden
the air is full of electric spirits, and we
rush out of our houses,
prancing in the reeling brightness
of our dealings, while up there
the artists of the sky, at last
awake after long apathy,
deliver their selfless performance.

10

We wonder anxiously
how we'll get down again
with our ludicrous air ships,
clumsy tin cans,
booming with nervousness—
unlike those gigantic nomads!
Desert shy they wander, lightly,
lentissimo maestoso,
above the ground,
drift along, unflustered,

and sometimes they gather
for palavers of great silence.
Then again they blow apart,
evaporate slowly high above,
and only a single cloud, small
as a yearning memory,
holds out, white, in the sky.

11

They are above mistakes.
No one will be quick to claim
that one of them is misshapen.
A minute-long shower
sends down millions of sleet flakes.
Every one is perfect.
No two flashes of lightning alike.
And all this without a brain!

Heartless/heartfelt, poor/rich, good/bad:
Those problems are alien to them.
Typhoons, deluges, hailstorms,
their wordless drama
means heartbreak for some,
but looks different, very different,
to the speechless admirer
watching from Ararat.

12

One moment of inattention,
and there they are, suddenly, white,
blossoming, indeed, but not very solid,
a bit of moisture, high above,
something imperceptible, melting
on the skin: rapid transition
from one phase to the next—all good and well.
But even the physics of clouds
is not entirely in control.
In case of doubt 'it is assumed',
'one is of the opinion'. They are opaque,
those broken rainbows, virga,
columns of light, halos. Heaven knows
how they do it. A separate species.
transient, but older than our kind.

And it will survive us by
plus minus a few million
years, that much is certain.

Translated by Esther Kinsky